AROUND THE TRACK

RACE CARS THEN AND NOW

AROUND THE TRACK

RACE CARS THEN AND NOW

Steve Otfinoski

BENCHMARK BOOKS

MARSHALL CAVENDISH
NEW YORK

Benchmark Books
Marshall Cavendish Corporation
99 White Plains Road
Tarrytown, New York 10591-9001

Library of Congress Cataloging-in-Publication Data
Otfinoski, Steven.
Around the track : race cars then and now / Steve Otfinoski.
     p.   cm. — (Here we go!)
Includes bibliographical references and index.
Summary: Surveys the world of race cars, from their early years to the
cars and races of today.
ISBN 0-7614-0608-5 (lib. bdg.)
1. Automobiles, Racing—History—Juvenile literature. [1. Automobiles,
Racing.] I. Title II. Series: Here we go! (New York, N.Y.)
TL236.084   1998   796.72—DC21   97-11548   CIP   AC

Photo research by Matthew J. Dudley

Cover Photo: *The Image Bank,* Alvis Upitis

The photographs in this book are used by permission and through the
courtesy of: *Photo Researchers, Inc.:* G. Ashendorf, 1, back cover;
Jean-Marc Loubat, 6-7, 12, 13, 14; Tom Burnside, 9 (bottom), 11;
Bernard Asset, 19; Patrick Behar, 23; J.P. Lenfant, 24; Patrick Vielcanet,
25; Dingo, 32. *The Image Bank:* Walter Bibikow, 2; Reinhard Eisele, 15;
Tom Williamson, 16-17; Alvis Upitis, 17 (inset), 20, 27, 30;
Jacques Cochin, 18; Franco Villani, 21; Eric Meola, 22; Janeart, 26.
Corbis-Bettmann: 6, 8, 9 (top). *UPI/Corbis-Bettmann:* 10.
Reuters/Corbis-Bettmann: 28, 29.

Printed in the United States of America

6 5 4 3 2 1

To Brett and Kaitlin,
who like the fast lane

Race cars are built for speed.
Whether whizzing around a track,
over narrow city streets, or across
a rocky desert, race cars are the
fastest things on four wheels.

No sooner were automobiles invented than
people started racing them.
The first race cars were ordinary automobiles
that raced on public roads.
The race pictured above took place in 1894
between the French cities of Paris and Rouen.
The drivers in the race on the opposite page
were all women.
The Marmon Wasp (below) was the winner of
the first Indy 500 race in 1911.
How do you think this race car got its name?

Early European auto races were among the most
glamorous in the world—and still are today.
The 1937 Coronation Trophy Race (above) was held
in London and covered 140 miles.

In the 1920s and 1930s, race cars were among the best designed and sportiest of automobiles. This Bugati built in the late 1920s had large tires, sleek lines, and a custom-made dashboard. It also had 125 horsepower, so it could really fly down the track.

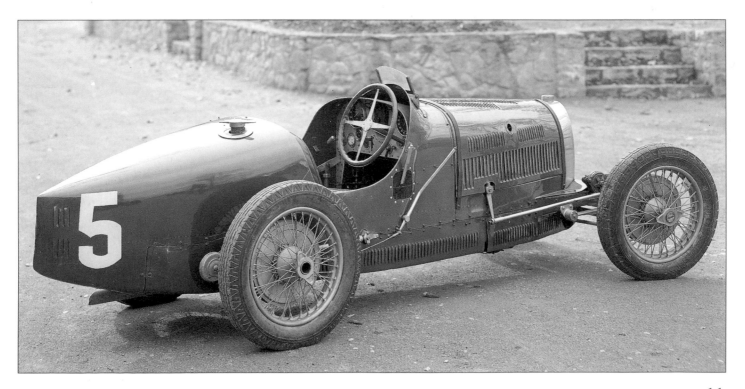

Today, the Grand Prix is the cream of car races.
There are actually fifteen Grand Prix races held each year
all over the world.
The one in the tiny European country of Monaco (above)
is perhaps the most famous.

Here is another Grand Prix race in Detroit, Michigan.
Each race is 150 to 200 miles long.
The first car to finish the required number of laps around
the course wins.
Points are awarded in each race, and the driver who wins
the most points wins the World Drivers' Championship.

14

No two Grand Prix cars are exactly alike.
But they all have certain features in common—
an open cockpit, one seat for the driver, and a
rear engine.
Grand Prix race cars can go over two hundred
miles per hour.
Drivers must go fast on the straightaways and
then slow down on the curves.
It takes skill, nerves of steel, and luck to win
this challenging race.

The Indy 500 is the most popular auto race in the United States.

More than three hundred thousand people crowd into the Indianapolis Motor Speedway every Memorial Day weekend to watch this thrilling race.

Drivers race around a 2 1/2-mile track.

The first driver to finish two hundred laps, which equals five hundred miles, is the winner.

Everyone who races gets a share of the prize money— over $8 million.

Car racing is an exciting but dangerous sport.
The cars are going so fast that it is easy for
drivers to lose control.
In one split second a car can skip the track,
spin into the air, and land on top of another
car, causing a pileup and possible injuries.

Stock car racing is very popular in the United States.
Stock cars look like ordinary automobiles on the outside.
On the inside, they have powerful engines that make
them go fast.
Many stock cars, like the one above, are covered with
colorful decals, numbers, or other marks to identify them.
Fans can spot their favorite driver and car and cheer
them on.

Drag races don't "drag" at all.
In fact, they are usually over in six seconds or less.
Dragsters race two at a time on a quarter-mile drag strip.
Some of these cars go so fast, a parachute pops out of
the rear to help them stop after crossing the finish line!

Karts are small, heavy-duty cars that can go almost anywhere.
A cross-country kart race is something to see.
Karts scramble up rocky hills and down dusty gullies.
Karts are great for kids.
Some kids are kart racing before they have learned how to
ride a two-wheel bicycle.

A car race is a thrilling experience—for both the drivers
and the fans.

The cars zoom down the track when the green flag is waved.

If a car has a problem, the driver pulls it over for a pit stop.

The pit crew works quickly to repair and service the car
and get it back in the race.

Every second counts.

The cars zoom round and round the track.
Then it's time for the final lap.
One car pulls out in front of the others.
A man waves the checkered flag as the first
car crosses the finish line.
The winner!
The race is over and the crowd roars.

The winner is the hero of the day.
But for the other drivers, there is
always another race.
Race cars are fast, furious, and fun!

INDEX

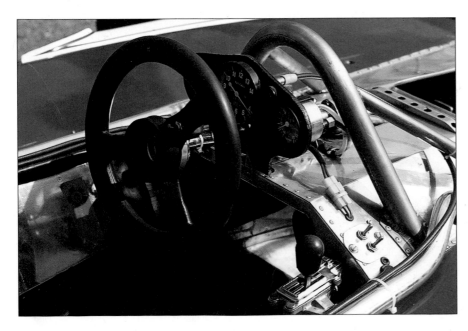

FIND OUT MORE

Cave, Ron and Joyce. *What About? Racing Cars.* New York: Gloucester Press, 1982.

Italia, Bob. *Go-Carts.* Edina, MN: Abdo & Daughters, 1994.

Knudson, Richard L. *Racing Yesterday's Cars.* Minneapolis, MN: Lerner Publications, 1986.

Wilkinson, Sylvia. *Kart Racing.* Chicago: Childrens Press, 1985.

STEVE OTFINOSKI has written more than sixty books for children. He also has a theater company called *History Alive!* that performs plays for schools about people and events from the past. Steve lives in Stratford, Connecticut, with his wife and two children.